The Story

Written by Lynn Nicol

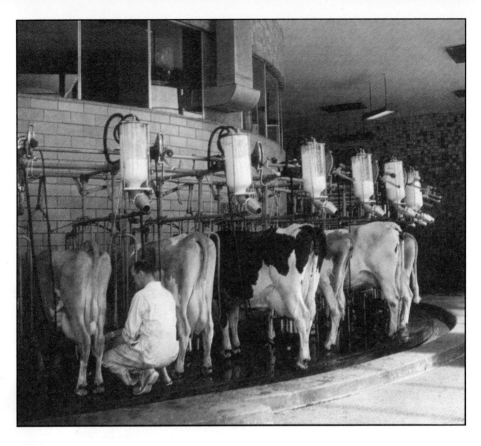

The farmer takes the milk
from the cows.
He uses a milking machine.

The milk goes into
a refrigerator truck.
It goes through a hose.

A machine cleans the milk.
It takes out all the germs.

A machine puts the milk
in jugs.
It puts the lids on too.

Another refrigerator truck
takes the milk to the store.

People buy the milk
and take it home...

for children like me to drink!